The History of
YSTRAD MYNACH Boys and Girls Club
1936-2006

Published with the support of Awards for all Wales

Old Bakehouse Publications

Abertillery

© Maldwyn Griffiths and Richard Herold
is association with
Members of Ystrad Mynach Boys and Girls Club

First published in September 2006

All rights reserved

The right of Maldwyn Griffiths and Richard Herold
in association with
Members of Ystrad Mynach Boys and Girls Club
to be identified as authors of this work
has been asserted by them
in accordance with the
Copyright Designs and Patents Act 1993.

ISBN 1 874538 98 0

Published in the U.K. by
Old Bakehouse Publications
Church Street,
Abertillery, Gwent NP13 1EA
Telephone: 01495 212600 Fax: 01495 216222
Email: oldbakehouseprint@btopenworld.com
Website: www.oldbakehouseprint.co.uk

Made and printed in the UK
by J.R. Davies (Printers) Ltd.

All rights reserved.
No part of this publication may be reproduced, stored in a retrieval
system, or transmitted in any form or by any means, electronic,
mechanical, photocopying, recording or otherwise, without
the prior permission of the author and/or publishers.
For the avoidance of doubt, this includes reproduction of any
image in this book on an internet site.

British Library Cataloguing in Publication Data: a catalogue
record for this book is available from the British Library.

Foreword

I am honoured and privileged to be asked to write the foreword to this history of Ystrad Mynach Boys and Girls Club.

My association with the club goes back many years. My late mother-in-law, Mrs Eileen Harmon, was Leader of the club for about 25 years.

Clubs like this one make a very important difference to the quality of our lives. They help to provide young people with a sense of self-worth by organising useful and interesting activities. Adults that give up their time, often for no financial reward whatsoever, act as good role models for the club members. They help to make young people see themselves as useful members of their community. Young people are naturally energetic and creative. All too often we are ready to criticise young people for inappropriate behaviour. Sometimes this criticism is justified but often the problem is caused by a lack of youth facilities and activities. Clubs like Ystrad Mynach Boys and Girls Club can make that difference.

This book traces the history of the club from its foundation in the early 1930s to the return visit of the *'Merseybeats'* in January 2005. It is full of interesting news clips, notes of meetings, reminiscences, and photographs.

The book records the role played by football and other sports. It talks about drama events and visits to far flung places like Cardiff and London. It recounts the visit of celebrities like the singer Frankie Vaughan and the Duke of Gloucester. There is also an account of a visit to London by club members to meet the cowboy film star *'Hopalong Cassidy'*, or William Boyd to give him his real name.

This book is a fascinating account of local enterprise, commitment and hard work.

The efforts of Ystrad Mynach Boys and Girls Club have been recognised by a large award from the 'Big Lottery'. This investment will allow the club to expand its existing services and consider new ideas. The future looks bright for the club and therefore for the current and next generation of local young people.

As that future unfolds, it is important that we remember all those that helped to bring it about. This book is an excellent and permanent record of the painstaking and selfless contribution made by so many people over all those years.

Jeff Cuthbert AM
National Assembly Member for Caerphilly
and President of Ystrad Mynach Boys and Girls Club

Contents

		Page No.
Chapter 1	History of the Club	6
Chapter 2	Trips and Outings	41
Chapter 3	Sport	53
Chapter 4	Awards	67
Chapter 5	Social Dances	75
Chapter 6	Opening of the New Hall	90

Introduction

The club has had a glorious past, and now it is facing a glorious future. The vision of its leaders and supporters has come to fruition, despite many obstacles and frustrations. A 'State of the Art' building, with all the facilities necessary to attract young members, to encourage them to participate in many diverse and varied challenges, led by a team of enthusiasts, and with the young members' needs at heart. As a correspondent of the *Rhymney Valley Express* I have had good relations with the club that will continue even more strongly, as the club moves forward. I have been privileged to have been invited to present trophies to the deserving boys and girls at the Annual Presentation Awards, and been able to write about events there and facilities including the inauguration of a young brass band. The club has always been involved in the community and every year representatives lay a wreath of poppies at the War Memorial in Ystrad Fawr, on its behalf. Young members have also taken part in concerts for charity and there has always been good leadership so that youngsters can enjoy themselves in a well ordered and disciplined environment. I hope to be writing about events that take place here and to have regular reports to include in the Ystrad Mynach Column of the *Express*. Good luck, best wishes and every success to you all.

Cyril Thomas

The funding for which the Club will be eternally grateful.

Ystrad Mynach Boys Club History

The groundwork for the Boys Club in Ystrad Mynach started in 1933, when Mr Isaac Pugh and Mr David Jones were involved in schoolboy and ex-schoolboy football. A committee was formed in a hut that was used as the Labour Party Hall at the station end of Lewis Street. It was later owned by Mr John and called the *John Hay & Corn Store* later to become the Unemployment Hall. There are glowing references to teams that were around in 1933 with the main leader and organisers Mr Isaac Pugh and Mr David Jones (Snowy). They started the school and ex-schoolboy soccer teams which were highly praised in the local papers. An extract from a newspaper dated July 7th 1934 reads - *'League Football - Mr D Jones presided over a meeting in the Workmen's Hall when it was decided to apply for entrance to the Rhymney Valley League. The officers elected were Mr D Jones Chairman, Mr Isaac Pugh Treasurer, and Mr Iestyn Owen Secretary'*. The earliest of these team photographs is that of the schoolboys' junior side taken outside Ystrad Mynach Junior School in the 1934-35 season, the date is clearly marked on the ball. At the time they were top of the Caerphilly Schools Soccer League. The earliest known photograph of a committee is marked 1933-34 and another marked 1936, when, according to records the Boys Club name was formed in the Unemployment Hall before moving to the Moose Hall, a corrugated shack in Lisburn Road where the club stands now. Some of the founder members were Isaac Pugh, David Jones, Mr DJ Jonathan, Mr Tom Brooks and Mr Davies the bank. One of the first boys to join the club and who became one of the most active members and a notable football player was Ken Pugh, the son of Isaac Pugh.

Schoolboys Soccer

Two extracts from a newspaper cutting on the 12th of October 1935 read,
Caerphilly Schools Soccer - Ystrad Mynach 5 Coedybrain Boys 1
The undefeated Coedybrain Schoolboys were visitors to Ystrad Mynach in a Caerphilly District League game. The first half was very even with both sides playing fast and steady football. G Hallett opened the scoring for the home side, but Coedybrain equalized quickly through W Earle. Ystrad Mynach were superior in the second half and goals were added by C Jonathon (2), T Meads and Merendhi. Meads at centre-half was in brilliant form and kept his forward line well supplied with accurate passes.

Ystrad Mynach ex-schoolboys v Abertysswg. In the ex-schoolboys Division 3 Ystrad Mynach boys entertained Abertysswg boys. Abertysswg won 5-3; Price for Abertysswg centre forward scored 3 goals and thus obtained the 'hat trick' two weeks in succession, Greaves and Morris obtained the other two goals. Mahon, at right half was in brilliant form Pugh was outstanding for Ystrad Mynach.

Apollo Boys Club

There is some confusion over the following paragraph that was taken from a newspaper cutting in April 1934 and clearly named the club as the Apollo Boys Club.

Boys Club Dance - At the Moose Hall on Thursday the Apollo Boys Club held a successful dance. Officials were chairman Mr D Jones, vice chairman Mr C Edwards, treasurer Mrs M Long, and Secretary Mrs Willie Evans with The Pratley's Dance Orchestra from Llanbradach in attendance.

Memories of some early members

Victor Davies a former Boys Club Member recalls some of his memories of those early years when the club was young and there was plenty of talent around and each wanting to express their own individual skills or as part of a team. It was the first club to start inter club matches with Onllwyn and Seven Sisters in Neath and Filton in Bristol something that the club is proud of in its history. The dances on a Saturday night were very popular and the resident band was Phil Amors OK Dance Band and were held in the Institute Dance Hall.

Apart from the success of the football teams the club had many other sporting teams that helped to build up the club's reputation and become a name that other clubs would come to admire and respect. There were some very notable players in billiards, winning many competitions adding more success and again giving the club a name to fear in all classes of sport. Boxing is a sport that is not recognised in today's clubs but Ystrad Mynach produced some excellent boxers. Table tennis was a club favourite with everyone wanting to play. Members raced to the club to see who could play the first match and how many opponents they could beat. The standard of play of the members was so high resulting in some long lasting matches. During the war years, such was the standard of the table tennis team that they won the East Glamorgan final.

Among other club activities were camping, discussion groups, film shows, gramophone recitals, competitive concerts and lectures. There were the usual boys' hobbies like woodwork, stamp and card collecting with boys building up huge accumulations.

The drama class became much talked about, as this was the club's main feature all year round, producing some outstanding amateur actors that captivated audiences whenever they performed. During the early part of the 1940s the producer Miss Bronwen Rees BSc was highly praised for her drama class by the playwright Mr Eynon Evans. The plays were very successful and were achieving many standing ovations for their performances each night. Haydn Webb was one of the drama class's most notable actors who had built up a reputation and was chosen to take part in the National Association of Boys Club travelling theatre in England and Wales.

Ken Lloyd a former member was one of the members of the drama class and recalled that on many occasions, most of the props needed for the plays were brought from the home of the club's leader Mr Isaac Pugh, then taken back after the play was performed throughout the valley.

In 1946 on the club's 10th Annual Meeting the committee accepted a challenge cup from WA Guppy who was one of the local butchers in the village. It was to be presented to the best performing boys club member every year. The committee faced having to decide what methods to adopt in selecting the best boy, but a satisfactory scheme was devised and the first winner was W Wittle from Cefn Hengoed. The cup still exists today and adorns the trophy cabinet in the club. Mr Isaac Pugh the club's leader and secretary, praised the committee that comprised of a younger group than previous years owing to the call-up of lads to the forces.

July 15th 1954
Hopalong Cassidy
cowboy idol of thousands of children,
will lead 48 American youths on a tour of Britain

It was an idea to promote British and American friendship and an exciting opportunity for 48 British youths to meet up with 48 American youths. *Hopalong Cassidy* screen star Bill Boyd and children's idol of dozens of cowboy films arrived in London on a goodwill tour of Britain, the 48 American youths were representative of every American State. Allan Rees from Penybryn and an Ystrad Mynach Boys Club member was one of four Welsh lads to be chosen for the 48 British boys. It was a memorable time for Allan who was lucky enough to have been picked for the tour. Highlights of the tour included a civic reception by the Lord Mayor of London, a welcome lunch at the Savoy Hotel and a tour of England, Scotland, Wales and Ireland.

In aid of Ystrad Boys Club funds

Bargoed Workmen's Institute
Amateur Boxing Show - Friday, September 28th 1956
Programme 3d each

Smallpox jab does not spoil John Cross' game

Although suffering from the after-effects of a smallpox vaccination, John Cross played well for Wales in the Boys Club international against England at Villa Park Birmingham.

Picture of the first committee taken around 1935 when it was Ystrad Mynach schoolboys' soccer and ex-schoolboys' soccer. Top row: Mr Davies, Mr Sprigs, Mr Weaver, Mr H Griffiths, Mr Lewis, Mr Jones, Mr Osborne and Mr I Lewis. Middle row: Mr WJ Probert, ?, Mr D Jones, Vicar Davies, Mr DJ Jonathan, Mr Rogers, Rev. DJ Williams, Mr Davies and Mr Isaac Pugh. Bottom row: Mr G Higgins, Mr L Smith and Mr V Greenaway.

One of the first known photographs of Ystrad Mynach Schoolboys' Soccer team taken in the grounds of the school and dated 1934-35. The schoolboys and ex-schoolboys were always near the top of the Caerphilly and District schoolboys' league and finished top on many occasions. Some of the schools played were Twyn, Trethomas, Coedybrain, Cwm-Aber, Hendre, Aber mixed, Llanbradach, Rhydrie and Senghenydd. The ex-schoolboys played such teams as Markham, Abertysswg, Nelson, Penybryn Pals, Dowlais, Trelewis, Graig Hengoed, NT Thistles and Fochriw.

Some of the club's members pictured here in 1939, as they wait for their turn in a club tournament of table tennis. Ernie Hamer, Gordon Evans, Ken Brown, Tom Thomas, Graham Watkins 1 and Graham Watkins 2.

This photograph is quite interesting as it shows an old hay barn that was near the clubhouse as the table tennis championship is underway

With the table tennis championship finished the snooker tournament is about to begin as the players take time out for a group photograph at the back of the building in 1939. In the top photograph are Al Jones, Frank Greenaway, Tom Thomas, Howard Evans, Gordon Evans and George Higgins. In the bottom photograph are Ken Pugh, Ike Pugh, Ken Evans, Howard Evans, Harry Green and Glyn Jones.

One of the earliest group photographs of the members that shows the club building. The corrugated shack was formally the Moose Hall and home to the Boys' Club until fire destroyed most of it on March 4th 1960.

Pictured here are most of Isaac Pugh's family taken outside the farm in Brynmynach Avenue in the late 1940s. With the support of his family, his vision of a boys club was achieved going from strength to strength. Some of the names are Isaac, Euron, Elwyn, Josh, Hughie, Maria, Blodwyn, Alice, Lucy, Betty, Lily with baby Christine, Hazel with baby, Glanville, Annie, Audrey, Brenda, Tied and Gee, Mary, Olwen, Alwen.

During the 1950s the Duke of Gloucester paid a visit to the club on his South Wales tour of Boys Clubs. He was introduced to the club's committee members, with the Duke shaking hands with Mr Ron Walters. The Duke paid tribute to the club's leader, founder members and committee who had all worked hard for the well-being of local boys. He was shown the club's facilities that included a game of snooker.

During the Duke of Gloucester's visit he was shown around the club and given a PT demonstration to which he commented on how well they performed. He was also shown the art and craft section that included many objects from the plastic class where he saw some plastic brooches by club member Roy Dainton. The Duke of Gloucester was pleased with the high standard of workmanship and said it was a credit to the boys club.

Boys will be boys and this picture says it all. All boys love to play in mud as this picture was taken on what was called the mud bath (the club's football field). The club leased two pitches and this was one of them. When it rained the pitch turned into a lake and the boys had to go out before a match with buckets and spades to try and drain off the ground.

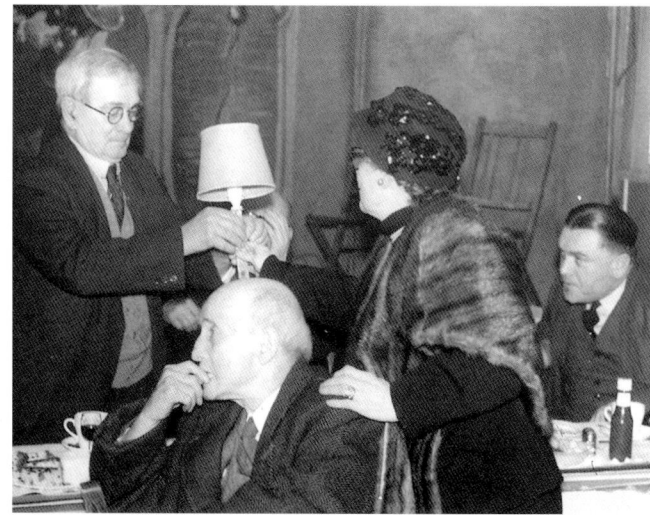

The Boys Club had some remarkable success in the field of arts and crafts with members gaining many awards in the Arts and Crafts Festivals. Many of the objects made for the festival were of high standard, winning the praise of all the officials who had to judge them, they commenting on the outstanding exhibits such as one of the table lamps shown in the picture on the right. The craft room was well equipped with various tools for woodwork, art, painting, plastics etc. as can been seen here.

Fire at the Boys Club - March 4th 1960

On March 4th 1960 a fire broke out at the club and within two hours a furious inferno desolated the building and left 160 young members without a club. It looked as if the club was finished, but with the dedicated help of the management committee (almost all of whom were former members) the boys distributed an appeal for urgent funds to help them replace their building. The boys made the following leaflet asking for donations and that an adult helper would call shortly. Or, a simpler way to help was to write your name on back of the leaflet and pin a ten shilling note to it and drop it in the National Provincial Bank, The Square, Ystrad Mynach. Through organised dances and house to house collections the boys raised £2,500 towards the cost of the new building costing £11,000, giving the boys of Ystrad Mynach the finest headquarters in Wales.

The following article was taken from a newspaper cutting showing how other clubs rallied around to help.

Ystrad Mynach Boys Club which was striving to raise funds to replace the burnt out headquarters, was given a boost by several Welsh clubs helping out. These clubs were by no means well off but rallied around to give support. The latest clubs to help have been Troedyrhiw, Newbridge, Hirwaun, Treharris, Ystrad Rhondda, the Wrexham group, Welshpool, Nantymoel and Giants Grave. In addition Swansea Boys Club has made a gift of a billiards table and Ynysybwl and Cardiff Central Clubs hope to help.

Minutes of the Management Committee
March 8th 1960

A meeting of the Management Committee was held at the top floor of the Co-operative Butchery Department Ystrad Mynach March 8th 1960.

Mr DJ Jonathan was in the chair.

Also present were: - Mr Sanderline, Mr R Walters, J Jones, H Hussey, Mr H Jones, W Hamilton, Mr and Mrs Cockram, J Brownsword, W Dainton, H Brooks, Mr Evans, L Hussey and R Cross.

Tonight's meeting was mainly held to discuss two points

1. To report on a fire that had broken out at the Boys Club at approximately 11pm on Friday 4th March 1960 thus destroying the main hall and partly damaging the bottom floor; two fire engines were called to the scene.
2. The second was to discuss the future of the club under these circumstances.

Mr DJ Jonathan asked Mr H Jones to give a report on what happened last Friday. Mr Jones said nothing unusual had happened on Friday, just that he had closed the club at the usual time at 9.15 pm; he was called from his home by the police to go to the Club. He said that the police had reported that someone had broken into the building from the time the club was closed to the time of the fire. Saturday morning Mr Jones had found that the clock was missing from the billiard room and that packets of potato puffs was found on the floor of the committee room. Mr Jones said that these were not there Friday night as he went in the committee room just before closing the club to shut off the gas heater; if they were on the floor then he would have seen them. Eventually the clock and some crisps had been found in the club surroundings. The police had taken all evidence with them and the matter was left entirely in their hands.

Mr Jonathan said that we could not discuss whether we were going to have a new building at this stage, until the insurance people had stepped in and the WABC had made their appeal for us.

Mr Sanderline moved that a letter should be sent as soon as possible to the Electricity Board asking them to rewire the bottom part of the club and a copy of this letter be sent to the insurance company so that when this was completed the boys of the club could carry on there for the time being, this was agreed.

It was agreed that Mr Jones and Mr Hamilton should approach the Workmen's Hall and the Church Hall to see if we can carry on the Thursday night dance, and that the cheapest quote be accepted.

Mr Brownsword reported that it was difficult for him to contact the boys for their football matches and that he had a full programme in front of him. This again showed the importance of getting them together at the club.

It was agreed that a bus be granted for the under 19s football team who were playing at Merthyr on Saturday.

W Hamilton confirmed that the Welsh Sports had given the club a dartboard and a set of darts after hearing of the fire. It was agreed a letter of thanks should be sent, also a letter of appreciation to be sent to Mr Graney for allowing us to hold our meetings at the top floor of the Co-operative Butchery Department.

Correspondence was read and dealt with and bills passed on for payment.

Mr DJ Jonathan then declared the meeting closed.

Welcome back

A meeting of the of the Management Committee was held at the Boys' Club on Tuesday 28th June 1960.

Mr Brownsword was in the chair and members present were Mrs F Cockram, W Dainton, H Jones, J Jones, W Hamilton, Mr Isaac Pugh, Mrs J Brownsword, H Brooks and R Cross.

Mr J Brownsword welcomed Mr Isaac Pugh to the meeting, after his long illness. Mr Pugh said he would like to take this opportunity to thank all those concerned for keeping the club going under the difficult strain, with the fire and the absence of himself. He said that he might be back at the club within the next week. Mr Brownsword speaking on behalf of the committee and the members said we are looking forward to seeing Mr Pugh back to the club once again.

ARE WE DOWNHEARTED ?

Under 16 Winners Rhymney Valley Boys' Clubs Football League, 1958-59. Undefeated.

Winners, League Cup, 1958-59.

Semi-finalist, W.A.B.C. Cup.

... YES, since 4th March ...

when two short hours of furious fire desolated the building which **for twenty-six years** had been the home of the **Ystrad Mynach Boys' Club.**

The Club is the oldest in the Rhymney Valley. Many grown men, now the fathers of families and successful in life, owe their early training to the influence of the Club. Members have won high honours in national and international sport, and the Club has a fine reputation for friendship and character-building which is recognised far beyond the borders of Wales.

TWO HOURS OF FIRE HAVE BROUGHT A QUARTER OF A CENTURY'S WORK TO A STANDSTILL

. . . . . . but this work must go on ! **There are One Hundred and Sixty young members at the moment who need the club** the only alternative is the street corner.

THIS CONCERNS YOU — will you please help?

With the help of their management committee (almost all of whom are former members), the boys are distributing this appeal for urgent funds, to help them replace their burnt building. An adult helper will call on you shortly—please be as generous as you can.

OR, A SIMPLER WAY TO HELP. Write your name and address on the back of this leaflet, pin a 10s. 0d. note to it, and drop it into the National Provincial Bank, The Square, Ystrad Mynach. Mr. T. A. Evans, the Hon. Treasurer, will write and thank you.

The boys of today . . . . are the MEN of tomorrow. Don't let them down !

Work is underway as these two photographs show the laying of the foundations looking towards Central Street and the other showing the structure of the hall nearly complete with the corrugated club in the background.

Management Committee Meeting
Tuesday May 25th 1961

Mr Isaac Pugh said that the following boys were to be congratulated for doing well in the Boys Club of Wales Arts and Crafts Exhibition in Cardiff.

Alf Brownsword	6 first and 4 seconds
Denis Jones	2 first
Roger Woods	1 first

Congratulations to the following teams for winning the following competitions in the football season.

Open Age -
Winners of the Victory Cup
League Champions

Under 18s -
Winners of the Boys Club of Wales Cup
Winners of the League
League Champions

Under 16s -
Runners up in the League

Management Committee Meeting - June 27th 1961

Mr DJ Jonathan explained that Mr Isaac Pugh was unable to attend tonight's meeting owing to another serious illness, the Committee wished him a speedy recovery.

Advertise for a new leader

At a Management Committee meeting held on Tuesday August 15th 1961 it was agreed that Capt. Glynn Jones go ahead and advertise for a new Club Leader due to the continuing illness of Mr Isaac Pugh who would be retiring in October after 25 years in the job.

Plans for the Foundation Stone of the new club

At a Management Committee Meeting on September 12th 1961 it was agreed that the foundation stone be laid by Mr D Jones our first chairman and for nineteen years, a life member of the club and one of the founders. Mr Jonathan said that Mr Jones deserved this honour owing to the great deal of voluntary work he had devoted to the club. It was also agreed that Mr DJ Jonathan our present chairman and Mr I Pugh our Club Leader should have their names engraved on the stone. Mr G Webb is to arrange for the actual wording.

A special Meeting of the Management Committee Friday October 6th 1961

Tonight's meeting was specially to interview Mr Peter Thomas the applicant for full time Club Leader.

After a preliminary discussion, as a result of which, it was clear that all members present favoured the appointment of Mr Peter Thomas, on the following agreements.

1. Housing - It was explained that the local housing position was no better than it was elsewhere. The members promised to exercise such influences as were possible and to assist in every way over temporary accommodation. Mr Thomas expressed a preference for residence in the district if possible and would be prepared if necessary to spend an initial period in apartments.

2. Salary £750 per annum, rising by annual instalments of £36, one final instalment of £40, to a maximum of £1000 per annum.

3. Superannuating. It was agreed that arrangements would be made for superannuating.

4. Notice. One month's notice to be given in writing by either side.

5. Commencement of service. November 1st 1961.

6. Mr Thomas is 21 years of age and married, and recently successfully completed the youth service diploma course at University College Swansea, and has been a voluntary worker in the Boys Club of Wales for a number of years. Until recently was honorary secretary of Swansea Group of Boys Clubs. He is a keen footballer and impressed all members present.

Sad Loss of a Great Leader

A meeting of the Management Committee was held at the Boys Club on Tuesday November 21st 1961. Mr DJ Jonathan was in the chair:

Also present were Messrs P Thomas, A Cross, J Brownsword, H Brooks, H Jones, D Perring, W Hamilton, R Cross and Mrs J Brownsword.

Before the commencement of tonight's meeting a minute's silence was held in memory of our ex Club Leader Mr Isaac Pugh who passed away at his new home Penpedairheol on November 9th 1961. Mr Pugh was buried at Ystrad Mynach Church on Monday November 13th.

Leaders Report

On Friday November 10th a service was held in memory of Mr Isaac Pugh conducted by Mr Thomas, some 80 members attended and went very well. A wreath was sent on behalf of the Management Committee and boys. The six bearers at the funeral were all present members of the club.

Opening of the New Club - October 9th 1962

On October the 9th 1962 the new club was opened and Sir Maynard Jenour, president of the Boys Clubs of Wales, performed the opening ceremony with Mr Cliff Morgan, a former Welsh rugby international unveiling the commemorative plaque. Rev EJ Lawrence blessed the stone. The local Member of Parliament brought the proceedings to a close with his wish *'may this club be a monument to its founders, and the means whereby the village may be kept together. May the boys who frequent it enjoy many happy hours, and learn this lesson of living together'*. Following the unveiling, a buffet was laid on for all guests. A visit by singing legend Frankie Vaughan was part of the opening week.

Membership had increased and with the new hall made it possible for more pre-match training. The new building had a comfortably furnished lounge and was to become the senior lounge and chat room. Many decisions were made in this room about the future of the club and new activities. As Peter Thomas recalled *'from that humble beginning, we were able to go on a series of adventures, which took us from a horse-drawn canal barge in the Midlands to a holiday in Europe. We still have holiday tales to tell. We booked our twenty places on that canal barge and arrived late one evening full of pleasurable anticipation after a noisy bus journey. Calamity for us, joy for the boys. We discovered too late that the barge had forty berths and guess what, the other twenty were taken up by a girls club from Manchester. On the Belgian trip the boys discovered five seated bikes. It's unbelievable what havoc forty Welsh boys and eight bikes can cause.'* (The Ostend Police were very understanding.)

The Management Committee
of the
Ystrad Mynach Boys' Club
request the pleasure of the company of

_____

at the Opening of their New Club Premises
on Tuesday, October 9th, 1962 at 3.00 pm
by Sir Maynard Jenour, T.D., D.L., J.P.
(President of the Boys' Clubs of Wales)
and the Unveiling of a Commemorative Plaque
by Cliff Morgan, Esq., BBC Personality

Peter Thomas,
3 Aneurin Bevan Avenue,
Gelligaer,
RSVP *Hengoed, Glam.*

From the ashes a super Boys' Club

From the ashes of the movement's original building, destroyed by fire two years ago has arisen at Ystrad Mynach, one of the most modern boys' club premises, costing £11,000 in the Welsh mining valleys. The new building symbolises the enthusiasm of a membership of 105 young people led by an energetic management committee alive to the need for facilities, which such a club can offer. For the past two years ever since the original premises were burned down, the club has carried on its work in temporary premises still to be continued to be used on the spot where the fire occurred.

Towards the £11,000, club members themselves have raised £2,500 - £500 short of the £3,000 target they set out to collect.

Fifty per cent of the cost has come from the Ministry of Education and twenty per cent from the Glamorgan Education Committee.

All sections, the management and the members have played a great part in raising the money. Mr Peter Thomas the club's full time leader and the youngest qualified leader in the Boy's Club movement in the British Isles told me.

'It has been a tremendous job,' he added.

The club is known on many parts of the Continent as the result of members' trips abroad and joining in international camps in this country.

Several members in recent years have obtained 'caps' for their country in junior football and recognition for their achievements in other forms of sport.

Just over ten years ago the Duke of Gloucester in the course of the tour in South Wales visited the club.

Of the 16 members of the management committee, 12 are former boys of the club a fact, which Mr Thomas states, has contributed greatly to the success of the club.

Picture taken at a recent reunion of the members, left to right Paul Hughes, Paul Jones, Peter Thomas and John Edwards.

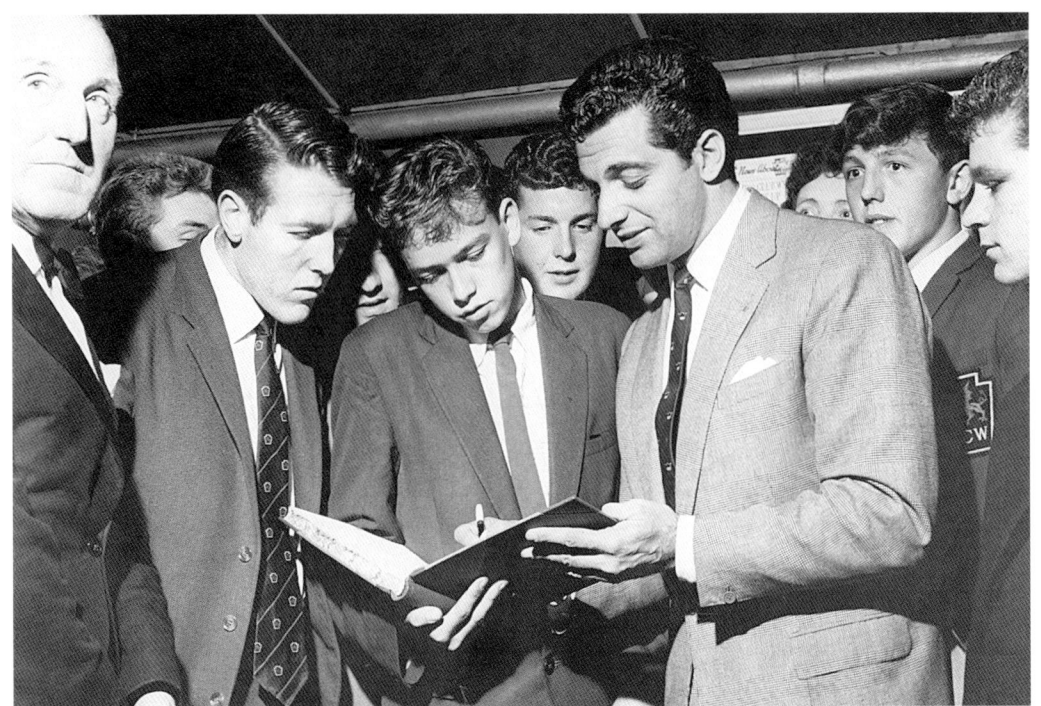

Singing legend Frankie Vaughan visited the club during the opening week of the new premises as part of his fund raising tour of boys clubs in South Wales. He raised more than £1,000 for St Athan Boys Village after visiting Ystrad Mynach, Pontypridd and eventually St Athan. On his arrival at the club he was asked to sign in by Boys Club member Idris Penrose, with Mr Peter Thomas (leader) Mr Guppy, Roger Williams, Michael Rice in the picture.

Frankie Vaughan admiring the miner's lamp Boy's Club member Michael Rice presented him with. During his tour of the new £11,000 club he made a short appearance on stage singing his new hit song 'Hercules'. Also in the picture are Len Huzzey, Peter Thomas, Mr Guppy, Clive Jones, Joan Cross and Mrs Brownsword.

With the new club opened and membership increased, regular discussions were held concerning the well being of the club. The idea was to get members more involved in being a part of a team. In the words of former club lead Peter Thomas 'Through our activities we built up a web of personal relationships which enabled us to motivate our members and to think about themselves.' *That relationship can be seen in these two photographs showing Mr Hayden Brooks talking outside the club with members and the other with the club leader Mr Peter Thomas debating with members in the committee room dubbed the* 'chat room.'

Newspaper cuttings around early 1960s

In co-operation with the Boys Clubs of Wales, the Ystrad Mynach Boys Club has adopted a child in Kenya. The boy, Gitari Mbol Nyaga, an eleven year-old who is deaf and dumb and depended on his grandfather, was picked up by police half-starved in the streets of Nairobi. Gitari has now been adopted by a school for the deaf in Nairobi and is supported by donations from the members of the Ystrad Mynach and other Boys Clubs in Wales.

Keeper takes a plunge

Ystrad Mynach Boys Club goalkeeper, Robert Lancastle saved his side from a Welsh Youth Cup replay with Swansea Town last Saturday and was nearly drowned in the process.

The swollen river skirting the Boy's Club pitch had already claimed three of the four footballs the teams started with. When the last ball was booted into the raging water, goalkeeper Lancastle stripped off his jersey, shorts and boots and dived in. Lancastle lobbed the ball back onto the pitch but was swept downstream before being rescued by other members of his team.

A club official said *'Robert certainly saved the match because we had no more footballs left it would have been abandoned if he had not saved the ball'*.

Ystrad Mynach fullback David Thomas scored the winning goal three minutes from time to put Swansea out of the cup. Robert Otten equalised for Swansea after Glyn Bishop had given Ystrad Mynach the lead. It was the second successive season that Swansea has been put out of the cup by the Rhymney Valley side.

April 1964 - Boys Clubs Arts and Crafts Festival

The Welsh Arts and Crafts Festival sponsored by the Boys Clubs of Wales was held at the Ystrad Club on Saturday, the first time in the Rhymney Valley.

Councillor Howell Edwards chairman of the Gelligaer Urban Council who opened the festival commented on the outstanding exhibits and the high standard of work submitted by the local club. He congratulated the leader and the committee on the high standard after the club had received 63 awards, the highest number ever received by the club in the festival.

The Awards

Trevor Court obtained three silver awards for craftwork and his trolley was selected as the outstanding exhibit in the whole festival. The chairman of the club's members committee, Geoffrey Williams, obtained the only silver award for written work.

Other silver awards were gained by Brian Hart for writing a short story, Peter Nicholas, Maldwyn Thomas, Ken Pritchard, Howard Jones and a group effort from the plastic group. All these awards were for craftwork. Fourteen-year-old Phillip Mills gained two silver awards for art.

Bronze awards were gained in art, written work and crafts by Michael Vaughan, Phillip Mills and Alf Brownsword for art; Trevor Court, Lyn Hegarty,

Keith Garbutt, Maldwyn Griffiths, Cliff Pritchard, Stephen Mathews, Robert Pask, Howard Jones, Keith Williams, Michael Caple and Geoffrey Williams.

The following received commended awards: Brian Barron, Michael Caple, Maldwyn Thomas, Phillip Mills, Lyndon Hughes, Malcolm Herbert, Cliff Pritchard, Stephen Mathews, Phillip Fry, Eric Moore, Keith Garbutt, Geoffrey Preston, Robert Pask, Alan Jenkins and Geoffrey Williams.

John Edwards

British triple jump champion John Edwards is seen here at the Montague Burton Sports Ground in Leeds and on his way to the Boys Club National Championship at Crystal Palace the following year.

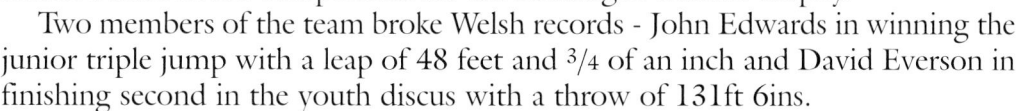

Boys Clubs News

Showing much improved form is the athletics team of the Ystrad Mynach Boys' Club captained by British triple jump champion John Edwards.

In the Welsh Boys' Club athletics championships at Jenner Park, Barry, the team finished sixth in the competition for the Montague Burton Trophy.

Two members of the team broke Welsh records - John Edwards in winning the junior triple jump with a leap of 48 feet and 3/4 of an inch and David Everson in finishing second in the youth discus with a throw of 131ft 6ins.

Billy Beer finished fourth in the final of the 100 yards. John Edwards was placed third in the long jump and fifth in the 100 yards. Dennis Jones was fourth in the mile and third in the two mile event. In the javelin, he finished sixth while David Everson was fourth. Other club athletes to reach the finals were Keith Parker and Roger Thomas.

Football

Fifteen year old Brian Prosser son of Mr and Mrs Mervyn Prosser of Nelson one of the club's leading soccer stars, left this to become an apprentice professional with Bristol Rovers youth team.

Brian, a former pupil of Graddfa School, netted 75 goals for the club in between playing for Bristol Rovers Youth team.

Club leader Peter Thomas said: *'Brian has the makings of a first class footballer,'* a feeling endorsed by Bristol manager Bert Tann.

Table Tennis

In the final of the East Glamorgan doubles table tennis championships the club team of Trevor Court, David Walters, Marilyn Morgan and Helen Jones defeated Abertridwr YMCA.

In the County finals the same team representing East Glamorgan were narrowly defeated by the Pontypridd Youth Centre team.

Road Race

Although well ahead for most of the five-mile road race, the club team was defeated by Pontlottyn County Youth Centre in the final of the East Glamorgan county road race.

David Everson, Alan Hayter and Lyndon Williams gave the Boys' Club a commanding lead after one and half miles. Howard Jones and Keith Garbutt continued the good running to give the club a twenty-yard lead at the halfway mark. On the return home Maldwyn Griffiths, Alan James and Tony Honeywill ran well but a mile from home, Pontlottyn took the lead and although Michael Vaughan and captain Roger Thomas made the effort, Pontlottyn were the victors.

Boys' Club Quiz 1964

The large hall at Ystrad Boys' Club was filled to capacity on Wednesday for the first annual quiz competition of the East Glamorgan Group of Boys' Clubs.

The questions were compiled by Mr Alan Morgan the Ystrad Mynach Boys' Club physical education instructor and the evening was organised Mr Peter Thomas.

During the evening the audience was also entertained to some delightful singing by the Girls Choir of the Ystrad Mynach Boys' Club under their conductor Mr Telfryn Thomas.

Cycling

Following instructions received by Mr H Stevens, the road safety organiser for Wales, a number of committee and senior club members have qualified as national cycling proficiency scheme instructors.

Snooker

After a brilliant day's snooker, Dennis Jones was declared the junior champion of the Boys' Clubs of Wales after a tournament at the St Athan Boys' Village. Dennis Jones was chosen for Welsh youth team February 12th 1965.

Most important news in the local youth activities was that of Dennis Jones, of Ystrad Mynach, Boys' Club, who has been selected to play for the Welsh FA Youth team against Ireland at Caernarfon on Saturday.

Because of this exciting news I am holding over my report on the Festival of Drama until next week. Devoting my article this week entirely to this young man who has brought well deserved honour to himself, to his town and to his club.

Table Tennis

Trevor Williams, Brian Harris, Michael Rice, Roy Chapel, Jeff Rees and Idris Penrose (Captain) represented the club in the match with the Gelligaer Church Guild. The club won by four matches to two.

Chris Sharp who was the Boys Club Leader after Peter Thomas left to take up a new appointment with Swansea Education Authority. Chris is seen here at St Athan Boys Village in 1965. Some of the names are Peter Reynolds, Glen Carlow, Glyn Davies, Brian Clifford, Dave Thomas, Andrew Morris, Phillip Price, Gareth James, Chris Sharp (Club Leader), John Davies, Glen Rees, Robert Evans, and Steve Jones.

At an early age Chris left Abertridwr to live in Swansea where after attending Swansea Technical College, he tried various jobs before accepting a housemasters post at the Turners School in Oxford. It was from here that Chris attended Liverpool University and successfully completed the full time youth leaders course before being appointed leader of the Ystrad Mynach Boys Club. An instructor in the Duke of Edinburgh Award scheme, Mr Sharp was also member of the National Boys Club, and a former member of Swansea Boys Club.

Mrs Harmon from Hengoed was to replace Chris Sharp and her involvement started after buying a raffle ticket for the club. Mrs Harmon was told how desperate they were for a new leader and would she mind giving a hand until they had a replacement for Mr Sharp. After helping out around the club she was encouraged to take out a youth leaders course and passed with flying colours. In 20 years at the club she became known as simply H or SUPERGRAN and loved to share a joke with the members. Mrs Harmon was to become one of the first female club leaders to be awarded the Silver Dagger that was sponsored by Wilkinson Sword for best club leader; chairman Trevor Whittle nominated her for the award. One of her many highlights was when Prince Richard, Duke of Gloucester visited the club on his tour of South Wales Clubs. The tour brought him from Georgetown, Troedyrhiw to Nelson and then to Ystrad and was greeted by many who lined the streets to get a glimpse of him. While at the club he tried his hand at table tennis, pool etc. and congratulated Mrs Harmon on her recent success of the Silver Dagger Award. Mrs Harmon is seen here with Mr Fred Evans M.P., William Norman, Councillor Turner, Mr Allan Rogers (then County Councillor later to become M.P. for Rhondda) and Terry Hennessey.

Prince Richard, Duke of Gloucester unveils a plaque in 1986 to commemorate the 50th anniversary of the opening of the Boys Club. This was one of the highlights of Mrs Harmon's time as Club Leader as he congratulated her on her recent success of the Silver Dagger Award. The little onlooker is Louise Walters.

Mrs Harmon is seen here during Presentation night in the 1980s and always known as simply H.

Gareth Williams took over from Mrs Harmon in 1990 and quickly encouraged others onto the management committee. As an established football referee he was often dragged into to referee games and unknowingly being inched into the role of club leader. With the help of other parents of club members they quickly set out to encourage new members from a wider area. Gary Field was elected chairman and over the next few years that proved a good decision, with Gary helping to drive the club forward. Other parents of club members were elected on the management committee, Tony and Tommy Greenaway, Chris Lewis, Roy Johns, Paul Bowley, Tony Honeywill and Ken Pritchard. A girls netball team was established by the chairman's wife Jackie Field and her sister Gaynor. Karate was introduced to the programme and outdoor pursuits to the agenda. This started to attract more girls and so the time had come to change the name to Ystrad Mynach Boys and Girls Club. The club was now being filled with new and interesting activities, which had not been seen in the club before. The 100-mile canoe race was one such event that took place on the Severn and Avon rivers. The event was a test in which young people had to paddle 100 miles over four consecutive days. It was a Spring Bank Holiday in 1991 and the first time that girls were introduced to the event. With over 500 young people attending, Leanne Berrill was to become the first girl at the age of fourteen to successfully complete the canoe test. During the next few years there were trips to Dublin, Edinburgh and Bolton. In 1995 Gareth thought it was time to move on as he had been offered the opportunity to become the full-time manager at Mountain Ash YMCA. Throughout his time at the club he enjoyed great support from parents including taking teams to matches, and supporting fund-raising activities.

Members can be seen here pictured outside the club prior to their departure for Ludwigsburg in Germany. They can be seen wearing their new jerseys displaying the Boys Club logo.

From left to right: Tony, Gareth, Stephanie, Cowen, Silvia, Ryan, Ken, Clare, Lauren and Michelle.

Kenneth Pritchard took over as leader of the club in 1995 after years working alongside the outgoing leader Gareth Williams. Ken was a Boys Club member during the 1960s, a keen footballer and played in goal for the club starting with the under 14s, 16s and finally the under 18s. Tony Honeywill (Secretary) has worked alongside Ken and given him full support throughout some difficult times at the club. Although Tony never played football for the club, his claim to fame was while playing as a reserve for Bargoed YMCA he scored his only ever goal against the Boys Club. They both remember some funny times at the club and a little story they can't forget was the smashed window. It was during a five-a-side kick around in the gym and someone - no names mentioned kicked the ball and smashed one of the windows. An angry Len Hussey stormed and said 'what header done that' a reply came from a very apologetic member and said 'it wasn't an header Len, I kicked it'.

There have been three flooding disasters in recent years with the brook at the back of the club overflowing and causing considerable damage inside the building. Ken recalls being called to the club for the third time and wept at the hard work they had done in just finishing off the restoration. One of the firemen at the scene who was pumping out the water jokingly asked Ken would he mind going outside, as fast as he was pumping out the water your tears were filling the place back up. The highlight of Ken and Tony's time at the club is a massive grant from the Lottery Fund that will help transform the building, giving it disabled access with lifts to the computer room, the refurbishment of the leisure hall and a new addition in the form of a brass band. It was all down to hard work in securing the grant and with the help and support of Glenda Genner of GAVO development officer for Bargoed it was made possible.

Members of the club can be seen here in 2004 and include three visitors from overseas who thought highly of the club and the kindness of its members towards them.

Monopoly will never date and will always be a favourite with members Stephanie Winwood, Coral Bruford, David Griffith, Laura Harding, Nicole Griffith as seen here in the top photograph. With the ever-growing need to adapt to modern technology the club installed a state of the art computer room in what used to be the old committee room. It is open four days a week and Michelle Donovan tutors a computer class on Tuesdays and Thursdays and members are quick to want to learn from basic to more advanced. In the picture are Liam Horley, Michelle Donovan, Clare Pritchard, Lauren Chapman, Laura Harding, Rhiannon Stone and Ryan Pritchard.

Michael Edwards, Dean Thomas, Robert Jones, James Hurley, Ian Jenkins, Jamie Williams, Nathan Edwards, Oliver Howells, Ashley Meredith, Daniel Kingdom, Nathan Thomas, Shane Oates, Gareth Jeffreys, Shaun Doonan, Craig Morgan, Arran Humphries and Dai Hurley.

Ryan Wood, Shaun Loxton, Keith Jones, Andrew Gomer, Simon Jenkins, Geraint Thomas, James Tucker, Tanner Davies (Manager), Paul Metters, Chris Bridaux, Lyndon Wangiel, Richard Moore and Graig Nash.

The Brass Band Section

The Beginning by Jonathan PS Whatley
When Colin Ash and I began to discuss bringing a brass band back to Ystrad Mynach we already had the instruments and a small amount of cash from the old town band, all we needed were premises. We approached various establishments in the village and realising that this was going to be an expensive operation hopes began to fade. However, one night in October 2004 we met Ken Pritchard in the Boys Club and as he welcomed us with open arms, the new organisation was planned. To much acclaim and fanfare the Ystrad Mynach Boys' and Girls' Club Brass Band Section was born on the 26th of January 2005.

A Bit of History by Colin Ash
Compared with other parts of industrial South Wales brass banding came rather late to Ystrad Mynach. The earliest was Penallta Workmen's Institute which flourished in the inter-war period. After the war, with the nationalisation of the mines, it took more than twenty years for the sound of brass to echo through the community once more.

Utilizing the old instruments of the former Penallta band, a local music teacher, Graham Baraar formed a band in the local Graddfa School. Under Ieuan Morgan this band achieved fame on a national level and its members went on to found, in 1982, a senior town band called Ystrad Mynach and District Brass Band under Alan Rowe. This band enjoyed success qualifying for the National Finals five times in the first 10 years until the end of the nineties when it folded.

The Tutors

Jonathan PS Whatley - Musical Director
Jon has played cornet and soprano with a range of bands in the South Wales area. These included the Ystrad Mynach, Lewis Merthyr, Bedwas Trethomas & Machen (BTM) and Newbridge Celynen bands. After studying for a degree in music, he is in his final year of training to be a music teacher and, alongside his hard work here in Ystrad Mynach, tutors with the Hibernian Club Brass Band in Mountain Ash as well as playing trumpet and keyboards in a successful soul band.

Piers Hallihan - Assistant Musical Director
On moving into South Wales in the late 90s, Piers joined the Ystrad Mynach Brass Band; when the band folded he moved to play for Mid Rhondda in Tonypandy and for the Byron Jones Big Band in Caerphilly. He currently plays bass trombone for the Abergavenny Borough Band.

Matthew Poole - Beginner Tutor
At 13 years old Matt was already a member of the Ynyshir Welfare competing band, and after juggling rugby, banding and a successful career in avionics he moved to Ystrad Mynach in 2005. Matt wanted to teach and the band needed a tutor, his experience has been well received and he has had a great impact on the younger players.

The Future
The future for a brass band in Ystrad Mynach rests with a team of dedicated tutors and the support of the Management of the Boys' and Girls' Club. It is hoped that the band will enjoy a long and happy life bringing Brass Band music back to the people of Ystrad Mynach.

Trips & Outings

There is a buzz of excitement as these boys from the club wait patiently on Ystrad Mynach Station before beginning their camping holiday in Cornwall. The familiar basic suitcase made of compressed cardboard which was typical of most families can be seen with the boys and on the porters trolley. Camping holidays under thick canvas bell tents were always fun with plenty of outdoor games and sports to keep the boys occupied.

The Boys Village in St Athan became internationally famous as an activity centre for male and female residents and this is the very first photograph of Ystrad Boys Club at the camp in 1937. Mr Isaac Pugh who was always at the heart of everything can be seen in the picture. The bottom picture shows Trotman's Transport of Bargoed who were kind enough to transport their tents and everything they needed for the clubs camp at Porthcawl in 1939.

On the beach during 1947 camp at Weymouth are Ken Evans, Hywel Jones, Ernie Smith, Geoff Howells, John Buckland, Laurie Thomas, John Smith and Wally Whittle.

A memorable time in the club's history is when seven members attended the international camp at Porthpean near St Austell during the miners' annual holiday 1957 and being the only group from Wales. Six of them worked in local pits in the No 5 area - 5 from Penallta and 1 from Llanbradach. The Penallta lads represented their colliery when it won the soccer cup final the season before. Boys and Girls from six countries attended and the boys from the club had remarkable success in all areas of competitions. They entered the seven-a-side and craft sections winning both: they defeated Austria 2-1, Germany 10-0 and France 8-0. In the craft competition they scored 100% every day. At the international camp are B Digby, Isaac Pugh and P Blewett. Kneeling Derek Lewis. Front row G Williams, AS Rees, G Owen and N Palmer.

Both of these photographs show the meaning of working together and in the top photograph the boys can be seen carrying the water at the Weymouth Camp in 1948. The bottom photograph shows the weight of the Bell Tents as the boys struggle to unpack during the 1954 visit to St Ives Camp in Cornwall.

These two photographs show the boys full of smiles as they enjoy some of their outings. The top picture is of some of the club members waiting on Ystrad Mynach Station during a day's outing to Cardiff Castle in 1949.
The bottom picture is of some of the members posing by the Cornwall Youth Camp sign outside the Porthpean Camp in Cornwall in 1955.

There is a hive of activity going on with the boys just finishing off setting up camp at St Ives Cornwall. The boys are seen here assembling the Bell Tents that were so familiar and again transported to St Ives courtesy of Trotmans Removals of Bargoed. The picture below shows the meal queue after a full day's activities at St Ives Camp in 1955 with many hungry boys waiting patiently for the delights of the day.

Members of the Boys Club can be seen here with their leader Isaac Pugh, Hywel Jones and other officials of the club on a camping holiday on the Solent. There were no five star luxuries on this camping holiday as everyone was prepared to play their part in the vegetable preparation, cooking and washing up. The Bell Tents and cooking stove can be seen in the background of the bottom picture while the boys enjoy the day's meal. This was a memorable time for the boys who enjoyed all the outdoor games and sports with plenty of hiking around the area. During the evening there was the usual campfire sing-a-long with many of the boys bringing out their vocal and guitar skills with numerous funny tales to laugh about.

A slight bit of trouble with the old car on a return trip from Cornwall in 1951 but nothing to worry about said Mr Hywel Jones. The bottom photograph shows the members during 1951 at Camford Camp.

48

Idris Penrose and other members of the Boys Club can be seen here holding the Boys Club of Wales Cup they won during the early 1960s at the St Athan Boys Village. They are Idris Penrose, Dilwyn Evans, John Hughes, Brian Prosser, Brian Hart, Brian Rich, Les Davies, Ronnie Mee, David Everson, Maldwyn Thomas, Roger Ganderton, Gareth Silcox, Gerald Williams, Phillip Mills and Trevor Williams. In the bottom photograph some of the names are Alan Hayter, Jeff Rees, Adrian Anderson, Ronnie Mee, Gwyn Jones, Dennis Jones, Idris Penrose, Haydn Ruck and Roger Williams.

On arrival at the city of Ludwigsburg in Germany the Chief Burgomaster and other officials greeted them and welcomed them to their city. His Grace Duke Ludwig himself 'designed and built' the city, ruling from 1693 to 1733. Ludwigsburg is a vibrant city with a fine palace and just 3 hours from Stuttgart. The members stayed at one of the hostels in the city and enjoyed their stay. There was plenty of team spirit during the outdoor and indoor games, the bottom picture showing members with their German opposing team and coach Mr Gunter side by side with Ken Pritchard.

During recent years there have been trips to England, Scotland, and Ireland. The photographs here show the club's trip to Bolton and the excitement on the members' faces show they are having a wonderful time. Some of the members are Gareth Williams, Ken Pritchard, Tony and Tommy Greenaway, Jennifer Williams, Clare Jackson, Leanne Berrill, Rachel Anderson and Janine Hinder.

Another memorable time for the club was the Scotland trip and some of the members can be seen here outside the Coach House being serenaded by a lone Scottish Piper. The netball team can be seen here prior to a game during the Scotland trip. The girls are Leanne Berrill, Janine Hinder, Jackie Fields, Becky Fields, Lisa Jones, Kate Davies, Nicola ? and Jennifer Williams.

Sport

The club's first football team and winners of the South Wales Football competition. Included in the team were, one who received the D.F.M. in the war and sadly one killed. They are P Hamer (Trainer), R Williams D.F.M., E Humphrys, T Meads, A Jones, K Pugh D.F.M., C Jonathan, I Pugh (Leader), D J Jonathan (Vice Chairman), I Lewis (killed in the war), F Greenaway, G Bird (Captain), G Higgins, ? Smith, D Jones (Chairman), F Beech and L Lloyd.

Going through their paces in this photograph taken outside the Boys Club are the athletes who came runners up in the relay race at the South Wales indoor games competition in 1937.

The under 18s and winners of the Caerphilly and District Youth Football League Cup Competition in 1942-43 season. It was a miniature cup because of shortages caused by the Second World War. Pictured are Mervyn Prosser, Gideon Howells, Alec Hayter, William Norman, R Dyas, Ken Evans, B Hellins, Isaac Pugh, DJ Jonathan, Joe Jonathan, R Dawkins, Lionel Lloyd, Gordon Jones, Vivian Mitchell, Ron Whatley.

Mr Isaac Pugh and four proud members of the Boys Club Relay Team are seen here after winning the relay competition at the Troedyrhiw sports day in 1937.

Members of the Drama Class during the late 1940s early 1950s who are Jeffrey Howells, Noel Jones, ?, William Norman, Ken Evans, Vic Davies, Ernie Smith, Beryl Jones, Thelma Farnam, Joan Peterson, Bronwen Rees, Brenda Pugh, Barbara Bernard and Isaac Pugh.

The club's rugby team is pictured here during some memorable times when the club boasted three successful teams. Most of these players went on to play for Penallta.

Table tennis is an exciting sport and the Boys Club has produced some excellent players. The above team were Welsh Association of Boys Clubs Champions in 1941.

This photograph shows the club's team outside the club before they embark on their journey to Newport and play in a Cup Competition where they won the East Glamorgan Final.

The under 16s team photographed in 1960 they are J Brownsword, H Hussey, P Broadhurst, T Burton, K Brownsword, J Cross, J Harry, 'Snowy' Price (Ref), B Jones, G Williams, A Livingstone, R Williams and Dick Wilding.

Pictured here is the unbeaten under 16s soccer team of 1959-60 season, Rhymney Valley Cup Winners and League Champions. Clive Bartholomew, Howard Miles, Terry Burton, Mickey Kibble, John Cross, George Griffiths, Eric Lancastle, Rowley Williams, Peter Broadhurst, Alan Jones and Howard Davies.

Boys Clubs of Wales Champions 1959 under 18s who were first to win the championship, beating Treharris in the final. Back Row Isaac Pugh, Joe Brownsword, Mrs Brownsword, Clive Jones (Trainer), David Hughes, Jacky Griffiths. Cyril Griffiths, Geoff Jones, Hywel Jones, Ron Walters and Mr DJ Jonathan. Front Row Lionel Saunders, Frankie Gater, Len Hussey, Roy Cross (Captain), David Arthur, Winston Dainton and Billy Chandler.

Another successful team from the 1960s. David Thomas, Jeff Rees, Keith Williams, Robert Lancastle, Phillip Amos, Gareth Silcox, Brian Hart, Ronnie Mee, Alan Jones, Len Hussey, Paul Jones, Peter Thomas, Brian Prosser, Billy Beer, Paul Hughes, Mal Thomas and Howard Jones.

Brian Harris, Terry Burton, Ray Beech, Idris Penrose, Alan Williams, Alf Brownsword, Ken Davies, ?, Gary Williams, Rolly Williams, Trevor Williams, Len Fowler; Peter Thomas (Leader), Haydn Brooks, Brian Rich, Joe Brownsword, Michael Rice, Eric Darch, ? O'Connor, Ivor O'Connor; Peter Broadhurst, G Harris, Geoff Williams, Roy Dainton, Gary Rouse, Elton Hart, Eric Lancastle, Clive Bartholomew, DJ Jonathan (Chairman), Keith Godsall, Billy Jones, Clive Jones, John Cross, Dennis Jones, Winston Dainton, Billy Chandler; George Griffiths, Bernard Kibble and Roger Williams.

Peter Thomas, Dennis Jones, Hoppy Evans, Alan Williams, Graham Harris, Brian Harris, Mickey Thomas, Dillwyn Evans, Roger Williams, Mr Parry, Michael Rice, Haydn Ruck, Lenny Fowler, Idris Penrose, Geoff Williams, Brian Prosser, Trevor Williams, Brian Rich and Charley Vaughan.

The first Boys Club Team to enter the final of the Welsh Youth Cup. On the way to the final they beat the top two Welsh clubs Swansea and Cardiff City. Back row Len Fowler, Billy Beer, Dennis Jones, Graham Harris, Gareth Silcox and Haydn Ruck. Front row Alan Jones, Trevor Williams, A Rees, Howard Jones and Idris Penrose.

The field was known as the 'Mud Bath' and in the picture are G Williams, N Price, A James, R Meredith, H Ruck, K Fowler, D Kozlowski, I Penrose, R Herold, ?, D James, P Dainton and R Chappel.

The under 16s team photograph which was taken at Maesycwmmer School during the early 1960s seen are Peter Broadhurst, Brian Harris, D Evans, ?, Adrian Anderson, Dai Parker, Billy Beer, Jeff Rees, Dennis Lewis, Len Fowler and Tex Tucker.

The under 16s and under 12s soccer teams with officials in the late 1960s Mr O' Brian, E Rees, Gareth Hopkins, H Bird, A Morris, J Saunders, G Morgan, B Morgan, Mr D Harmon, Mr Carey (Chairman), M Hart, A Parry, P Roberts, W Gordon, M Court, D Hughes, C Williams, S Morgan, M Elliot, E Hatham, P Roberts, H Beynon and P Thomas.

This photograph was taken during a German Youth Club visit to Wales and club members are seen here with some of the visitors. The picture includes Paul Craven, Gareth Hopkins, Alan Evans, Mal Court, Howard Bird, Dilip Lalwan, Gareth Rees, Elwyn Rees, Billy Gordon and Tony Rees.

One of the sponsors of the 1980s was A.P.T Windows of Ystrad Mynach. The owner Mr Fred Cooper and his wife Mrs Olwen Cooper are seen here with one of the teams they had sponsored and some of the names are Steve Rees, Peter Watkins, Graig Hurne, Jason Hardcastle, Richard Ward and Karl Webber.

Other sponsors of the 1980s were Alan Griffiths Windows, Alan Griffiths, Andrew Caitlin, Lee Clark, Ron Jones, Kenneth Parry, Richard Richards, Mrs Ann Griffiths, David Parnell, Karl Davies, Gareth Whittaker, Neil Teconi, Martin Roe, Stephen Kent and Gareth Williams.

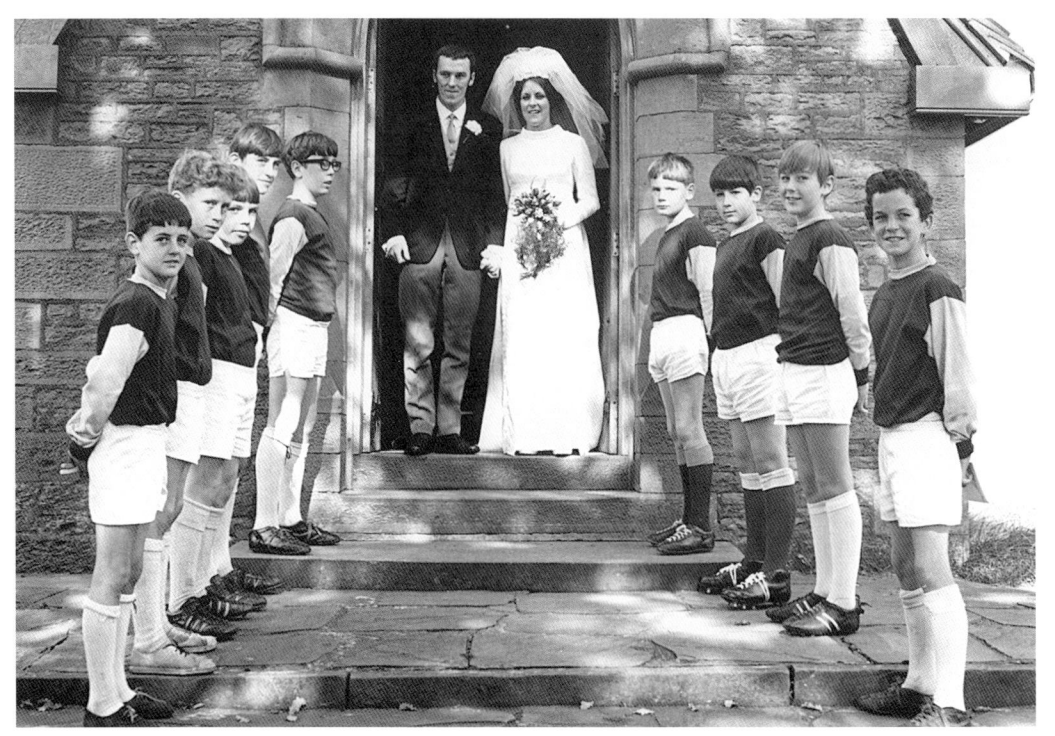

A very special tribute to their manager from the Boys Club under 14s who proudly line up as Mel Davies (Financial Secretary of the Club) and Pat Peters walk out together as Mr and Mrs Davies in 1969. The boys are Ian Batt, John Maslyn, Roy Tayers, Tony Rees, John Morgan, Gill Davies, ?, Andrew Morgan, Cyril Woods (Squish).

This photograph shows the successful under 10s 1988 Boys Clubs of Wales Champions by defeating Morriston 3-1 in the cup final at Ynys Park Ton Pentre. Damion Roach, Gareth Tucker, Stuart Lock, Rhys Hatfield, Lloyd Jenkins, Ian Shutt, Mark Price, Christian Murray, Lyndon Walters, Huw Brunt, Paul Davies, Paul Cheverton, Neil Clapham, Simon Walters, Martin Rowe and Julian Greenaway.

It was fun and laughter all the time at Bolton Boys and Girls Club and both teams are all smiles after a game of netball, some of the names are Rachel Anderson, Leanne Berrill, Claire Jackson, Lisa Jones, Jennifer Williams, Nicola ?, Janine Hinder and Jackie Fields

Wayne Morgan, James Rogers, Alex Krizan, Bleddyn Williams, Ashley Morgan, ?, Daniel Smith, Ashley Rowlands, Thomas Perriman, Ashley Griffiths, Richard Cox, Adrian Price, Chris Thomas and Piyar Puttharakas.

Under 15s 2005 Craig Bishop, Josh Mitchell, Ben Oram, Daniel James, Liam Horley, Rees Bullock, Dale O'Leary, Tom Clearly, Don Parry, Dean Marshal, Stephen Webb, Michael Eddinton, Jordan Humphries and Richard Snider.

Awards

Some early Boys Club trophies and shields are seen here with the Union Jack Flag wrapped around the base. For any sportsperson there is a vast range of trophies to choose from with one of the best well known right on the doorstep of the Boys Club. Everson Sports Trophies have been supplying the club for many years and part of their wide selection is shown here. The owner Trevor Everson and son Gareth are pictured with some of the staff, they are Jonathan Gay, Craig Beynon, Trevor Everson, Gareth Everson, Jayne Fletcher, Kelly Tudor, Nigel Beynon, John Cross,

After many years of excellent service to the Boys Club, this presentation is being made to Mr David Jones (Snowy) on his retirement in 1953 by Mr Isaac Pugh and DJ Jonathan.

This book would not be complete without paying tribute to the three founder members, Mr Isaac Pugh, Mr David Jones (Snowy) and Mr DJ Jonathan.

When they embarked on a venture in the early part of the 1930s to run schoolboy and ex-schoolboy football they had some vision of where they were heading, and by 1936 opened an Ystrad Mynach Boys Club.

There can be no greater satisfaction for them when they can see their own family taking an active part and helping to lead the way has they have done. Throughout this book there are references to many of their families with their involvement in sport, drama and supporting social evenings to name but a few.

The next paragraph is dedicated to the sons of these respected leaders.

Ken Pugh was one of the first boys to join the club and being in the schoolboy soccer in 1934-35 seasons. He was awarded the D.F.M. for countless acts of bravery under extremely difficult conditions during the war. The citation read Sgt. Kenneth Roydon Pugh, R.A.F.V.R.; a wireless operator has invariably displayed the greatest courage and devotion to duty. Mr Hywel Jones was to follow in his father's footsteps and became committed to helping young people of the area to lead a better and respectable life after leaving school. He was to become vice chairman and was highly respected by everyone. Hywel was a keen photographer and documented everything in detail. Were it not for Hywel's photography and the preservation of these photographs this book could not have been published or certainly not 96 pages. Mr Joe Jonathan was a noted rugby player and an active member of the club and participating in everything. He went on to become a member of the Management Committee and praised for his voluntary work auditing the clubs books etc.

Mel Davies

Mel became a member in 1959 playing for the Under 15s and then the Under 16s football team. He played for Tredomen AFC for a while before being enticed back by Hywel Jones to take up a coaching position. The Boys Club set Mel on the road to coaching and he eventually became the youngest Football Association 'A' Licence coach in Wales, coaching and managing in the Welsh League and working as a Regional Staff Coach with the FAW. Later to become full-time head of recruitment for a large American Soccer Camp company and from 1999 he also found time to work for Cardiff City's Academy as Coach and Coach Mentor where he is still employed part time, and currently working part-time for the University of the West of England in Bristol where he is Head Coach to the Football Department. Apart from a few years in the 1980s, Mel has coached at the Boys Club from 1967 to 2003, some thirty odd years.

Presentation night early 1970s with Mal Court, Curly Morgan, Gareth Hopkins, Paul Craven, Gary Capel, John Gateaux, Paul Thomas, Mike Elliot, Phillip Yorath, Nigel Beynon, Derrick Hughes, Colin Williams, Clive Mathews, Howard Beynon and Andrew Mulvey.

Mr William Norman standing in the centre presents two senior members of the Boys Club, David Walters and Alan Williams with tankards for passing their Youth Leaders course successfully.

Presentation night 1970s John Gatusch, Geraint Roberts, Nigel Beynon, Brian Aaron, Jeff Williams, Paul Shaddick, Mike Cooke, Nigel Hughes, Richard Colin Phillips, Mrs Jones, Clive Mathews, Gary Davies.

The beaming faces of Kim Davies, Julie Davies, Jan Bower and Elizabeth Morgan show how pleased they all are when picking up their badminton awards in 1974.

Presentation night with a guest appearance by Lee Baddeley of Cardiff City Bluebirds, Scott Thomas (Captain), Adam Lewis, Dewi Greenaway, Daniel Barwood, Dale Powell, Michael Morgan, Richard Veal, Robert Jones, Christian Jevatik, Owen Ashman, Ian Batten, Karl Rees, Craig Breeze, Jamie Williams, Cohen Griffiths.

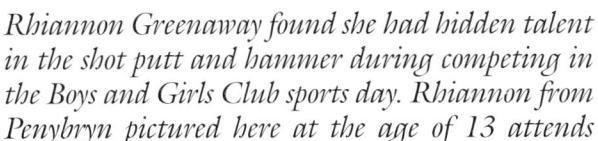

Rhiannon Greenaway found she had hidden talent in the shot putt and hammer during competing in the Boys and Girls Club sports day. Rhiannon from Penybryn pictured here at the age of 13 attends Lewis Girls in Ystrad Mynach and was a member of the club for many years. A proud moment for her was when she was pictured here with athlete Christian Malcolm and it has become a treasured memory for her family. After joining Newport Harriers she became East Wales Champion in the shot putt in 2001 and shot putt and hammer Champion in 2002 and is seen here displaying her Welsh vest and medal.

Helen Shirley from Penybryn joined the club in 1997 and competed in athletics for the Boys and Girls Club during 1997 to 2002 and winning a host of trophies, medals and vests; first competing against local boys and girls before representing the club at national level. Helen has a wealth of talent and specialised in the 100m, 200m, long jump and javelin. During 1997 and 2002 she was selected to represent Caer/Merthyr in athletics winning medals for 100m, 200m, long/jump, triple/jump and girls relay team. To add to this array of trophies, medals and vests Helen was female club member of the year in 2000-2001 and club runner-up in both table tennis and darts in 2002. Helen is pictured in both of these photographs and is a fine example to the club and Lewis Girls School where she attended.

Over the years the club has produced some excellent cricketers with many gaining Welsh Caps. Craig Breeze of Hengoed is photographed here in his back garden in 1995 after gaining his Welsh Boys Clubs Cap. Craig was also a notable footballer and played Mid Field.

The Guppy challenge cup was reintroduced after 40 years on presentation night 2004 and was awarded to Ashley Morgan for his outstanding achievements in cross-country and football. He is a fine athlete who came first in the British Cross Country Championships and second in the Welsh 1500 metres. He received the Players Player of the year award and was also the manager's choice as footballer of the year. Clive Jones who was one of the last holders of the Guppy Cup had the pleasure of presenting it to Ashley.

Presentation night 2004 and Kenneth Pritchard (Club Leader), Tony Honeywill (Treasurer), are seen here alongside special guests of the evening who presented the club members on the year's achievements. From left to right they are Cyril Thomas, Ken Pritchard, Jeff Cuthbert AM (Club President), Tony Honeywill, Mrs Brenda Thomas, Clive Jones and Ashley Morgan.

The club's main hall was full to capacity as the end of season presentations took place in 2004, rewarding all who had given their services to the club in many varied sports. Trophies were awarded for all manner of sporting activities and proud parents applauded the recipients with enthusiasm and joy.

Social Dances

Organised dances were always a good way of revenue for the club and were consistently well attended throughout their existence. During the early years there were dance orchestras, then came rock-n-roll and beat groups in the 1960s.

One of the Management Committee members, Bill Hamilton was the Val Parnell of the valleys and had contacts all over the country. It was through these contacts he was able to book some of the up and coming beat groups. Bookings had to be made months in advance and by the time the acts reached Ystrad they were well up in the pop charts. Ystrad became well known as one of the dance centres of the valleys with many of the top groups playing in the village either at the church hall or at the Institute Dance Hall. Some of these well known names were The Merseybeats, Johnny Kidd and the Pirates, Brian Poole and the Tremeloes, The Mojos, Heinz, Twinkle, The Applejacks to name but a few, and most of them supported by a local band from Blackwood, the Vampires.

The Vampires were formed in the early part of the 1960s playing rock and roll and the new craze called beat that was becoming to be very popular around the country. It was during their first year that they were featured on the Welsh television programme Gorwelion and BBCs 'Discs-a-Go-Go' the sixties equivalent to Top of the Pops. One of their greatest moments was when they won a talent competition to find the best South Wales group beating a band called Tommy Scott and the Senators who later became the world superstar Tom Jones.

A memorable time for two of the club's own beat groups 'The Meteors' and 'The Stompers' was when they shared 1st prize in the Boys Clubs of Wales Music festival in Cardiff. The groups consisted of boys from Hengoed and Cefn Hengoed and represented Wales in the national auditions to find the beat groups to appear on the Frankie Vaughan show at the Royal Albert Hall.

Another notable singer and guitarist was Tony Anthony, who played many nights at the Boys Club during the 1970s and 1980s. Tony played with many famous artistes during his career and one of his highlights was with Tony Christie when he was at the height of his career.

One of the dances that some remember but would like to forget is when the club organised a dance at Porth in the Rhondda. It was around 1966 and the club wanted a venue for chart topping R and B group the Pretty Things, and decided on Porth. After checking out the venue, Bill Hamilton, Ashley Williams, The Bear decided to have a few drinks in the local and as soon as they entered the bar a silence fell in the room. After a few beers the barman noticed there was going to be trouble as the locals had banded together blocking the doorway, he quickly called in the local policeman. He was around 6ft 4in and weighing around 16 stone and walked in and said to the local boys any trouble and you will have me to deal with and they calmly went back to their seats. The night of the dance didn't get any better as the concert had to be abandoned as fighting broke out everywhere and police were called in from all over the valley.

One of Ystrad's most eligible bachelors Mr Hywel Jones is pictured here in the company of some delightful ladies during one of the club's Christmas Parties. Hywel was noted for his inspiration to all Boys Club members and showed great leadership skills but never wanted the limelight. To all who knew Hywel they would agree that he had the full respect and admiration of everyone and would have made a perfect leader.
No party would be complete without the famous Corona party hat that can be seen and worn by all in the bottom photograph.

The Vampires were formed in the early part of the 1960s and played support to many of the top acts that were put on by the Boys Club. The original line up consisted of Robert Ovens, Gerry Bray, Mike Davies and Bob Wilson, Gwyn Roberts is in the current group and had the pleasure of playing support to the Merseybeats.

Two original tickets of top act shows that were put on by the Boys Club during the early part of the 1960s. The first one is of the late Johnny Kidd and the Pirates and support act The Vampires, July the 7th 1963 at the Workmen's Institute. The second is of The Merseybeats and again supported by The Vampires now T.V. Personalities, January 20th 1965 at The Church Hall.

YSTRAD MYNACH BOYS' CLUB
Present
DANCING WITH THE STARS
Featuring HMV Recording Artists from
'Thank Your Lucky Stars'

**JOHNNY KIDD
AND THE PIRATES**

PLUS SUPPORTING GROUP
The Vampires

From 8pm to Midnight
on Wednesday, July 17th 1963
at the
Workmen's Institute Ystrad Mynach
Late buses
Admission 6/-

YSTRAD MYNACH BOYS' CLUB
Present
The Merseybeats
(Recording Artistes)

Supported by
The Vampires
(TV Personalities)

on
Wednesday, January 20th 1965
at the
Church Hall Ystrad Mynach

Dancing 8-12   Late buses

Admission 10/-

The Institute Dance Hall was famous for its maple floor and was the first dance hall to have that type of flooring in the valley. Many dance bands were to play there with such names as The Aneurin Thomas Collegians, The Pratley's Dance Orchestra, and The Phil Amors OK Dance Band. At the time of these photographs the hall was renowned for its rock-n-roll and beat groups and the place to be for jive and twist lovers.

A delightful photograph taken during a social evening at the club with Len Hussey later to become assistant club leader, Carol Kurl, Haydn Hussey, Christine Pugh the niece of Isaac Pugh and Margaret Morris.

The names recalled in this photograph are Pat Holton, Elaine Nicholas, Dorothy Porter, Ann Dunk, Janet Jones, Mary Andrews, Mavis Munkley and Margaret Morris.

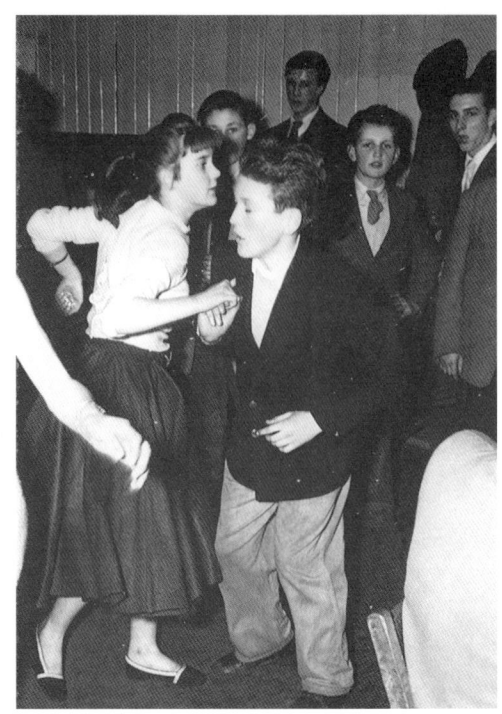

This set of four delightful photographs show the age of jive at its best. The first picture shows two of the girls who had worked so hard during the evening with the catering. Such was the enthusiasm of members and guests that as the music starts Joan Cross and her dancing partner have no time to take off their pinafore slips as they jive to one of their favourite records. The other three pictures show the art of jiving and at the time would have been dancing to artistes such as Bill Haley and Rock Around the Clock and Elvis's Jailhouse Rock.

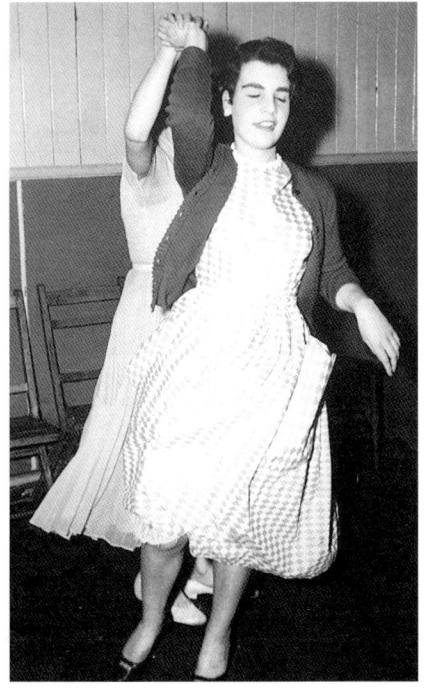

Some of the members get together for this group photograph they are Keith Godsall, Donald Joseph, Malcolm Howard, Ray Cross, Carol Taylor, Billy Chandler.

It is time now for the girls to have their group photograph taken they are Corrie Davy, Wendy Lewis, Joan Cross and Maureen Cross.

The social evenings were always well attended by the club's members and friends filling the hall to capacity. Some of the names recalled in this photograph are Jacky Griffiths, Michael Amor, Billy Chandler, Lionel Saunders, Clive Jones, and Donald Joseph.

Joan Cross can be seen here trying to serve one of the tables as the boys raise their cups (no alcohol as tea was the strongest beverage), as they are all eager to get in this photograph. Some of the names are Joan Cross, Dai Arthur, Dai Brooks, Winston Dainton, and Donald Joseph.

Singing legend Frankie Vaughan on stage at the opening evening of the new club with some of the faces being recalled such as Christine Pugh, Gloria Walters, Len Hussey, Val Penrose, Alan Livingstone, Diane, Teconi, Yvonne Hook, Jennifer Davies, Colin Cushing, Pat Davies, Carol Lloyd, Eileen Vernon.

One of the Boys' Club's own beat group were the Meteors from Hengoed and consisted of Geoffrey Holder vocals and rhythm guitar, Barry Jones lead guitar, Phillip Old on bass guitar and David Thomas on drums. They shared 1st prize with the Stompers in the Boys Club of Wales Music Festival in Cardiff and went on to represent Wales in Bristol to find beat groups to appear with Frankie Vaughan. At the music festival the Meteors won praise for their own instrumental composition.

Another of the Boys' Clubs beat group were the Stompers from Cefn Hengoed and consisted of Ken Pope on organ and vocals, Idris Ross and John Edwards on guitars and Clive Brooks on the drums. Along with the Meteors they shared 1st prize at the Boys Clubs of Wales Festival in Cardiff. At the music festival Idris Ross gave an outstanding performance in the National Piano Competition with his rendition of the Glass Mountain gaining a silver award.

Over the last few years there have been quite a few reunions taking place of past members and their friends who had all supported the club in many different ways. The three photographs shown here were taken during some of those reunions and their names are: Phillip and Sandra Lee, Malcolm and Ann Burgin, Robert and Belle Baxendale, Pauline, Ken, Susan and Teresa, John, Jeff, Lynda, Jill, Sue and Alan.

Time to share a joke and reminisce about the old Boys Club during a reunion of club supporters in the 1960s. The venue was Cascade Community Centre where some had met up for the first time in forty years. In the picture are Helena, Ros, Elaine, Jackie, Christine, Vicky and Ann. In the bottom photograph are Elaine, Brent and Collette.

YSTRAD MYNACH BOYS AND GIRLS CLUB

present

The 40th Anniversary return of

The Merseybeats

and

The Vampires

January 15th 2005 ✳ 7pm till late ✳ Admission £10 ✳ Bar

at **Lewis Girls Comprehensive School**

Lewis Girls School Ystrad Mynach was the venue for the return of the Merseybeats a well-known 1960s Pop Group seen here on stage during the night, with no shortage of people on the dance floor.

Pop history repeats itself after forty years when pop legends The Merseybeats and local legends The Vampires play together for a return visit to Ystrad Mynach. The photo shows the Merseybeats proud to display copies of two tickets shown 40 years apart.

Friends of the Boys and Girls Club celebrate the excellent news of funding for this book from 'Awards for all Wales'.

Bryn Meadows was the venue for this ex-members' reunion run by Howard Jones (Chippy) in 2005. It was a night of nostalgia reminiscing about the Boys Club. The night was worth all the effort that Chippy had worked so hard in putting together The picture below shows Nigel Beynon, Colin Kirkham, John Saunders, Paul Jones and Brian Morgan.

Opening of the New Hall

The highlight of Leader Ken Pritchard's time at the club was the opening of the new Leisure Hall on April 1st 2006. After a very lengthy time negotiating with all parties concerned and securing funding from The Lotteries fund and GAVO, the stress was worth it said a very relieved and proud Ken. Holding the club together during times of not being able to use the hall and the rebuilding was an anxious and frustrating period.

Ken and Tony pictured in the entrance to the newly refurbished Leisure Hall. The two plaques in the background are (top) from the National Lottery Funding Grant and (bottom) to commemorate the re-opening of the new hall on 1st April 2006.

During the day of the of the opening of the new hall, visitors were allowed the freedom of the facilities and pictured around the pool table are Karen Davies, Rhys Aitkenhead, Ellien Meara, Ethan Aitkenhead, Helen Turk and Jordan Davies.

Mr and Mrs Donald Roberts, Councillor Alan Angel Chair to Gelligaer Community Council, Christine Angel, Paul and Ann Davies Clerk to Gelligaer Community Council who were among the guests and speakers.

Leader of Caerphilly County Council, Councillor Harry Andrews and Jeff Cuthbert AM and President of the Boys and Girls Club, proudly hold the official opening plaque that brought much laughter to the hall. It was during the opening of the veil; the veil opened but there was no plaque to be seen (it had fallen down behind the stage). With bewildered looks from them both while looking at both sides of the veil that was now in Councillor Harry Andrews hands, he made a Tommy Cooper joke 'Just like that'. The audience fell about laughing.

The hall was full to capacity with civic dignitaries, guests, former members and family representatives of the founder members of the club, some of whom had travelled from Scotland and Cardiff. Families of two of the founder members David Jones and Isaac Pugh and long standing committee member Ron Walters pose together while browsing around the club's memorabilia, they are Professor Rhodri Jones and his wife Mary, Doctor Elin Jones, Christine Pugh and Gloria Walters.

Allan Rogers recalls the time just after the second occasion when fire had struck the club and funds were low and desperately in need of revenue. There was a knock on the door one evening and there stood Pat and Mel Davies who explained their concerns. Allan quickly set the task of finding new income for the club and the first place to start was the schools. They jumped at the chance of using the sports hall as it made sense, as the hall was not being used during the day. With revenue coming in on a regular basis the problem was solved. Allan can be seen here with old Boys Club members and pal Rolley Williams.

Margaret and John Edwards, Cohen Griffith the under 16s Manager, Allan Rogers Trustee, Pat and Mel Davies Trustee, are all proud to be part of the Boys and Girls Club past and present.

Old friends from the 1960's era of the club share a joke over some great times at the club they are Richard Herold, Alan Haytor, Brian Prosser, Idris Penrose, Howard Jones, Dave Thomas and Paul Hughes.

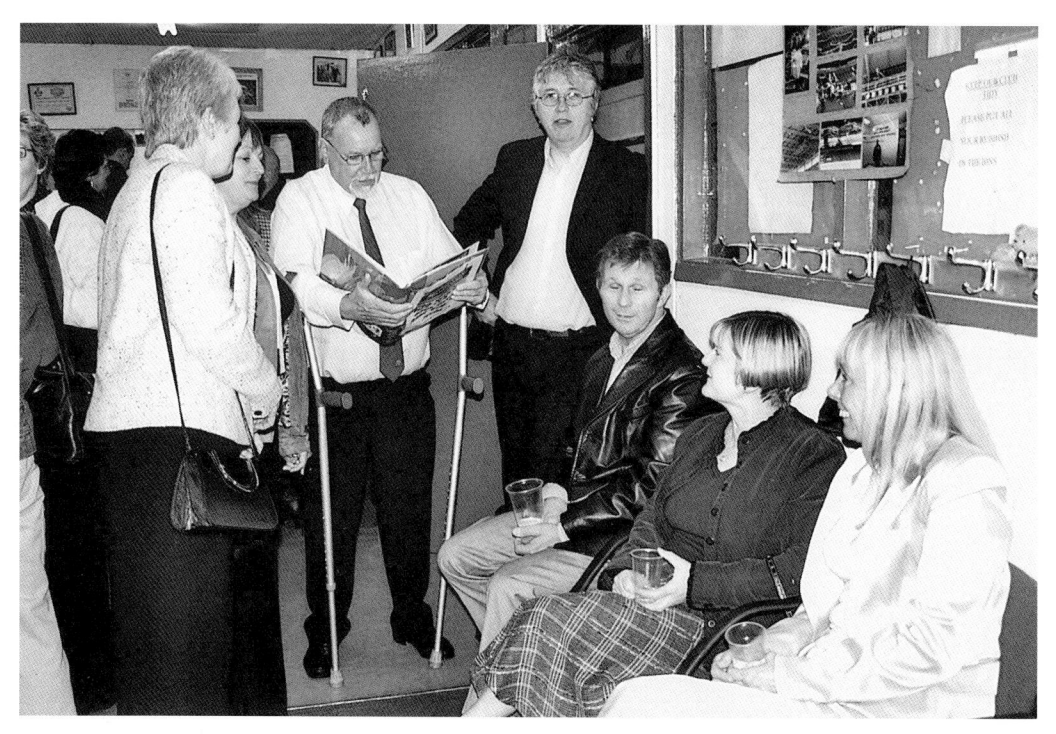

Clive Jones entertains some guests on the opening evening with some fond memories of his early days at the club during the 1950s and 1960s. They are Enid Reed, Marilyn Jones, Clive Jones, Steve Reed, David Jones, Janette Griffiths and Launa Herold.

Trevor Williams

Ystrad Mynach Boys Club was for me an ideal escape from the heartaches of life in a strict grammar school. Whenever I think of the Boys Club, I automatically compare it to my life in Lewis School Pengam because apart from family, these two institutions were dominant features of my adolescence.

At the Boys Club you had freedom to choose, from various sporting opportunities, you had the chance to discuss problems with keen caring adults. You were also able to contribute by belonging to the youth committee or by managing a younger team. You could go away for training weekends at St Athan Boys Village or you could go to St Austell for a Boy's Club camping holiday.

All the time you were taking part in the activities, you were increasing your personal and social skill in a way that was natural and enjoyable. Unfortunately this was in complete contrast to my experience at the grammar school where personal freedom, choice, socialisation were not part of the exam culture. This is why, for me the Boys Club was a haven.

My main memories were of beating Cardiff City, Swansea and Newport on our way to the Welsh Youth Cup Final. Obviously on a personal level, I was thrilled to be selected for the Welsh Boys Club and Welsh Schoolboys and and subsequently the Welsh Amateur side.

So many boys at the Club went on to achieve success in sport, many at international level and I am sure they would all mention the tireless contribution of people like Ike Pugh, Hywel Jones, Len Hussey, John Parry, Peter Thomas etc. These adults helped to create a great learning environment and this, allied to the great friendships that were forged at the Boys Club, helped the club to achieve a great reputation with the Boys Club movement.

When we hold re-union meetings we all comment on the far-sighted policies of the Club in helping us to develop as individuals within a competitive team structure. Whether this was by chance or by design I don't really know but generations of boys will be very grateful that it did happen.

Acknowledgements

Colin Ash
Janet Beynon, Craig Breeze
Jeff Cuthbert A.M.
Vic and Audrey Davies
John Edwards
Christine Davies, Pat and Mel Davies
Rhiannon Greenway, Maldwyn Griffiths, Jacky Griffiths, Cyril Griffiths,
Tony Honeywill, Richard Herold, Gareth Hopkins, Piers Halihan,
Gaynor Harmon, Dr Elin Jones, Gloria Jones, Howard Jones, Clive Jones
Mickey Kibble
Lewis Girls School
William Norman
Christine Pugh, Ken Pritchard, Pam and Idris Penrose, Mathew Poole
Allan Rogers
Scandinavian Design, Helen Shirley
Dave Thomas, The Merseybeats, The Vampires, Peter Thomas
Cyril Thomas, Gloria Walters, Lyndon Walters, Jonathan PS Whatley
Gareth Williams, Trevor Williams.

To anyone who has been inadvertently omitted, please accept our sincere apologies.